With all good wishes
Shelma Sessions

Ralph and Norma [?] [?]
in Natchez, May 14, 1984

Mississippi [?]

COUNTRY FOLK AIN'T SO BAD

This book is based on the persons and places I knew best. Names have been changed and events have been altered so as not to point a finger at anyone; on that ground it must be considered fiction.

COUNTRY FOLK AIN'T SO BAD

*Recollections of
the Old South*

THELMA SESSIONS

Exposition Press   *Smithtown, New York*

To my wonderful parents,
Eva M. and Walter L. Allred,
who firmly believed I was an unusually bright child,
although many were doubtful

FIRST EDITION

© 1983 by Thelma A. Sessions

ISBN 0-682-49956-0

Printed in the United States of America

Contents

Foreword

The setting of these stories is a small, very small town in the Deep South. There is a stately old court house, shaded by venerable live oaks, with down-drooping branches. There are shops, some large, some small, and when I used to come to the town there was a hotel. There were and are some old and beautiful mansions. Also, some very attractive smaller houses embowered in their gardens, where camellias and azaleas flourish to bloom in mild winters and early spring. Later, masses of roses are in full bloom.

In the not so distant past, an air of permanence pervaded the town, a gentle sleepiness. The streets were quiet, a few black people talked and laughed together, their voices soft, as they lounged on the sidewalk or draped themselves in a doorway while they waited for the bus. A dog was always on hand, dozing in the sunlight, looking mild and contented.

That was the town as I saw it when I came and went on the bus, and it was only a superficial view. Of course, where people are, there is always change and things always happen. Mrs. Sessions lived in the town for many years and has an intimate knowledge of the people, and what happened to them and why.

She pictures the place as it was, and with charm and humor, and sympathy tells the stories of men and women, both black and white, that she knew so well.

In these days when changes are so sudden and usually so drastic, most of us look back rather wistfully to the days that are no more and are hoping to meet the highly individual characters that come to vivid life in these delightful pages.

ALICE WALWORTH GRAHAM
Author of *Natchez Woman, Romantic Lady, Indigo Bend,* and many others

Look Back and Laugh

In the early part of the nineteen hundreds, I was born in Jackson, Mississippi, of wonderful, loving and proud parents. We lived on a short street in a good neighborhood sixty-five years ago but a terrible one now. The families on the street were all great neighbors and always ready to lend a helping hand. When anyone on the street was very ill the women took turns sitting up with the patient. Today they would think you were strange if you asked anybody to sit up with a sick friend.

Here in Natchez I have a friend, Ethel Roll, who lived across the street from us. We are the same age but when I say that, she always adds, "Yes, but you are six months older than I." I don't argue the point, but it is really only five months. We started school together in the primer and to this day she thinks I am stupid because I cannot remember who our second-grade teacher was. She is a great friend, a splendid church worker and has joined nearly every organization in town. She has two daughters and six grandchildren. She is too much of a Pollyanna but I love her dearly just the same.

Now, as I sit on this hill, in the best apartment Natchez has to offer, waiting to die from two unsuccessful hip operations because of a mugging in New Orleans, I enjoy looking back and reminisc-

ing. I live here because my only relative, my sister
Lois, lives just a few blocks away and is such a help
and pleasure to me. I would have gladly choked her
a week or so ago when she told the group with us
that she had heard Mom say she went to town years
ago when I was a baby and took me in one of those
old high baby carriages. The two biggest stores in
Jackson then were S. J. Johnson's on one corner,
and directly across the street was the other, Kennington's. She got to S. J. Johnson's and attempted
to cross the street to Kennington's. Capital Street
at that time was not paved, it was just plain
Mississippi mud. The baby carriage got stuck and
it took two men to carry me across the street. It's
such a pity I was too young to appreciate so much
attention. But with the bustling city Jackson is now,
I am sure the people who heard that story wondered
why I had not died of old age ten years ago.

This little street we lived on when my parents
first moved to Jackson was called Hunt Street. It
was in the days long before The Pill became so
prevalent and the street was alive with children.
There were several boys on the street and I bragged
I could out-run, out-climb and out-fight any of
them. Once, when my mother was having a committee meeting of her Circle at the church, a crowd
of us children turned over an old stove in the
alleyway far back of our house. Under the stove was
a nest of long crawling creatures. We put them in
the wagon and, as fast as we put them in, they
crawled out.

Not to be outdone, I picked up one in each hand
and, holding it by the tail, ran in the house to show
my mother. The ladies immediately saw they were
little snakes and rushed out of the house. My mother

shoved me toward the coal fire in the parlor and threw the snakes into the fire. I, however, had broken up the committee meeting. My mother often said her oldest daughter was very bad but her youngest was a very good child. I am sure her friends and neighbors thought that was the understatement of the year.

Across the street at the end of Hunt Street was one of the town parks. Dr. and Mrs. Reed lived in a lovely, big old house in one corner of the park. They had four daughters, two older ones, and, after an eight-year hiatus, had two younger daughters, Sue and Martha Bell. Martha Bell was Lois's age and Sue was my age and we played together constantly. Dr. Reed had bought the younger girl a stove one really could cook on. We fried potatoes every day and gave those that popped out on the grass to the boys and we ate the good ones. Each year the Reeds had a huge Christmas tree in Dr. Reed's study. One year just after Christmas, a crowd of us were playing under the tree and Mrs. Reed told us she was going calling and that we could play under the tree but not to light the candles. Those were the days before the beautiful little colored bulbs and we used tiny candles that fitted in holders that clipped on the tree.

We played for a while and then decided it would be more fun if we lighted the candles and nobody would know. We stood on chairs and lighted all we could reach and thought the tree was wonderful. All at once somebody noticed a piece of cedar had caught fire and, in the panic that followed, we shook the tree vigorously. In seconds the entire tree was blazing. We rushed to the parlor door where Corrinne, the oldest daughter, had her date, and tried to say calmly, "You better come quick, we think the Christmas tree is on fire." Never will I forget the look of horror on the face of the young man when he yelled, "Call the fire department quick, these damn brats are going to burn the house down!"

Mrs. Reed had gone across the street to see a friend who had a newborn baby. She had picked up the baby and walked to the window just in time to see fire and smoke coming out of the windows of Dr. Reed's study and the fire trucks driving up. She told my mother she could not remember what she did with the baby, but since I know of no terrible happening to a baby on the street, I am sure she gave it to the mother. The entire side of the Reed house had to be renovated due to water and smoke, but we never repeated that performance.

Sue was much more educated in the facts of life than Ethel and I. Never will I forget the look of disgust on her face when Ethel asked her if she ever looked at the babies in her Daddy's little black bag. She set us straight on that score. My sister Lois, who is five years younger than I, was born after I had prayed for several months for a little sister to play with. When she was one week old I rolled my wagon in and announced I was going to take her in the backyard where we were playing.

My mother was horrified and told me it would be a long time before she could go outside. I was thoroughly annoyed and left the room saying, "I wish I had never asked the Lord for a little sister as she ain't no fun." Venting my anger over this, I went to my mother's room, pulled a chair up to reach the top of the highboy, and got my mother's diamond engagement ring and swallowed it. Needless to say, there was great consternation and it took three days to recover the ring.

My family decided that the street across from the park was a much nicer place to live, so we moved there. Mrs. Reed had a friend from one of the nearby towns who often visited her, and after her husband's death, she came more frequently. Then—I am sure—a widow's grief was measured by the thickness of her mourning veil. Mrs. Gay, or Gaytime, as all the children called her, had a veil so thick that she paid Sue and me a nickel apiece to get on each side of her when she crossed the street so the streetcar would not hit her. We looked forward to her visits as we sometimes made the huge sum of a dollar if she made a long visit.

Our next-door neighbor, Mrs. Sutton, had no children and took up a lot of time with me. I adored her and when she took me places, I was really a paragon of perfection. My mother would hardly have recognized me—I was so good. She told me when Kennington's opened their tea room she was going to take me there and I could have anything I wanted. When the great day came, we went to the tea room and the waitress came to take our order. I asked for two olive sandwiches and a chocolate ice cream soda. Mrs. Sutton fainted often and she got so much attention, it was the dream of my life to faint. Unfortunately, nobody in my family has ever fainted, despite our trials and tribulations.

The grade school was just across the park from our house and my years there were fairly uneventful. My mother had an elaborately carved rosewood table with a marble top that sat in our parlor window. On it was one of the first old Tiffany lamps. When the lamp was turned on in the evening, it was the signal for us to come in and study our lessons. Since I was studying music at the Convent, I had to practice at least thirty minutes and then do my

lessons, have supper, take a bath and go to bed. My
mother never varied from that routine.

Grammar school was not particularly exciting but
when I got to high school I lived in another world.
There were lots of parties and lots of boys. I was
always madly in love with the last one I had dated.
Dick Taylor delivered the Jackson newspaper and
I have sat on our front steps for sometimes an hour
waiting for just one glimpse of him. My senior year
in high school I met Dick Sessions, or I should say,
Richard Andrew Jackson Sessions, and his good
looks and quiet, affable manner made everything
else fade away. He was graduated from college that
year and returned home to work. We were engaged
when I started college and we both wrote every day.
He waited for me to graduate from college and a
week after graduation, we had the church wedding
I had dreamed of for so long. After a brief honey-
moon, the only kind we could afford, we settled
down in the little country town his family had lived
in for generations. We lived a busy, happy life for
forty-two years until his death.

After my marriage, my sister went to Texas to
teach. My parents wanted to be nearby and they
bought property just up the street from us and built
a home. It was wonderful for us and, I hope, for
them also. After Dick's death, I went to live with
my mother as Dad `had died years before. My
mother lived only a year. I was so lonely that my
sister insisted I rent an apartment in New Orleans
as her husband was in business there. I had a lovely
time playing bridge and going to parties and was
one of the lucky few who were invited to join both
The Orleáns Club and Le Petit Salon the first year
I was in New Orleans.

I was going into the apartment house on St. Charles Avenue where I lived and, throttled by an unknown assailant, was thrown onto the concrete. This resulted in a broken hip. And now, since my brother-in-law has retired, he and my sister have moved to Natchez into the mansion his family has lived in for four generations. I live in an apartment four blocks away as I am unable to get along without their help.

As I sit in my apartment with so much time on my hands, my mind reflects back and I relive those years long since past. My friend Ethel fills in the areas I have forgotten. I had a wonderful family, the best husband in the world, and now, if I only could walk without help, I would be so very happy. But someday, maybe, I will climb "the golden stairs," my old cook, Hattie, sang about so many years ago.

The Gingerbread House

On the street across from the park where I grew up was a small Victorian house we called the Gingerbread House as it had such an ornate front for a simple little house. In it lived an old lady and her two old-maid daughters, Miss Helen, who was secretary to the mayor, and Miss Eleanor, who taught school. The old lady always referred to herself as Mrs. General Thomas A. Scott.

As children we were invited a few times to see the silver pitcher that sat on a marble top table just in the front hall. It had been presented to the general for some heroic deed and was engraved showing the dates, but we were never permitted close enough to see the engraving or touch it. It was more holy than anything on the altar at church. Mrs. Scott seldom left the house. The neighbors wondered whether she was guarding the pitcher or just did not want any contact with the neighbors. Mrs. Reed was the only neighbor who visited her and she did not go often.

When Sue married, she married a man from Richmond, Virginia, and moved there to live. Soon after Sue was settled in Richmond, Mrs. Reed went for a visit. When she visited the capitol in Richmond she looked at the roster of Confederate generals and she could not find General Scott's name. Her first impulse was to go to Washington and take the White House apart. But later she decided to wait until she returned to Jackson and tell Mrs. Scott she must go immediately to Washington and have this terrible mistake of leaving off General Scott's name corrected.

Soon after her return home, Mrs. Reed went to Mrs. Scott's and told her the terrible news. Mrs. Scott drew herself to her full height and said, "Mrs. Reed, my husband was a general in the Union Army." Mrs. Reed was stunned by the news and in Georgia sixty-five years ago nobody would have mentioned a relative who fought in the Union Army any more than they would have mentioned a relative in the penitentiary. Now that the succeeding generations think nothing of it, she would again be placed on the pedestal which she had put herself and be held in high esteem. Even my old yard man who had made a trip to Chicago told me, "That Smith and Wesson line ain't no more." The Mason-Dixon Line should never have existed.

Madisonville is, I think, one of the most truly southern small towns in the United States. We have exquisite pre-Civil-War homes and some pre-Revoluntionary ones. Even Sherman was said to have remarked when his troops came through that town that "These houses are too beautiful to burn." We have a pilgrimage every year and folk from every state in the Union come. Strange as it may seem, some of the same people come back every year. They love the Southern hospitality and warm greeting given them.

Being a Southerner and a Daughter of the Confederacy, a Daughter of the Revolution, and a Colonial Dame of the XVII Century, I am working on the requirements for membership in the Magna Carta Dames, but I have not gotten back past a vicar in England in 1524. My grandfather ran away at six-

teen and took his body servant with him to join the
Confederate Army. They knew he had lied about
his age so they kept the body servant and sent him
home to go to school. In a few months he ran away
again and that time they kept him.

His favorite story was of the reunion of the men
who fought in the siege of Vicksburg—both the
Union soldiers and the Confederates. One old Union
soldier was talking to another and said, "You see
at the foot of that hill, I took two Confederates."
Granddad said an old Confederate with a long white
beard and shaking his cane, rose and shook his
finger in the face of the Union soldier and said,
"You are a Goddamn liar—there's not a Yankee
living who ever took two of us at one time!" That
is the spirit which enabled the South to rebuild when
many of the men did not return while others,
wounded, came to homes that had been burned and
livestock destroyed.

We Southerners do not have the industry, the
universities and the money the North can boast of,
but we do have that indomitable spirit that has made
the South a beautiful land and its people gracious
and lovely. However, we are all alike, for the people I meet in Washington at D.A.R. and Colonial
Dames meetings are justly proud of their states and
their heritage and they, like us, are trying to hand
down to their children a better place to live than
they had inherited.

We have succeeded in making this *one* country
and truly *one* people with the same hopes, fears and
aspirations. Mrs. Scott in the Gingerbread House
would be lauded today unlike sixty-five years ago.
Sue Reed and her children and grandchildren still
live in Richmond and when we meet occasionally

in Jackson we relive those years when we were so happy and carefree.

In our neighborhood, three doors from our house, lived the Methodist minister and his family. He was a very sad, serious-looking man who gave one the impression that religion was anything but joyous. His wife was very domineering over him and their three daughters. One of the girls, Helen, was my age and we loved doing things together. One day we had planned something Brother and Mrs. Simms would have been horrified over had they known. We were eagerly waiting for them to leave as Brother Simms had a funeral to conduct. Mrs. Simms had ordered some face powder from the drugstore and she refused to let her husband leave until the powder came so she could fix her face properly.

We watched for the boy from the drugstore on the bicycle and finally he did come and the Simmses left for the funeral twenty minutes late. We knew Mrs. Sutton was afraid of cats and we had heard her say she thought she would die if she had to touch one. She kept big galoshes by the front door which she slipped on over her shoes every day when she went in the yard to check on her flowers. An old cat in the neighborhood just had kittens and we got two of the tiny little ones and put one down in each galosh. Sure enough, when she came out and put her feet in the shoes, she fainted dead away. They got the doctor but she stayed that way so long we thought we had killed her.

My mother's house was high in the back and we hid under the house, very quiet, frightened, bad little children. Those were the days of "The Perils of Pauline." This old serial ran every Thursday at the Istrione Theatre and on those days we raced out of school and ran down Capital Street to get to the first show. Each week poor Pauline was left tied to the railroad track with a train approaching or hanging from the limb of a tree by her hair. We lived from one Thursday until the next to see what terrible fate had befallen poor Pauline. Once on the coast at a banker's banquet, one very ill-mannered man was asking key questions of everybody at his table trying to guess their age. When he got to me I said, "I go back to 'The Perils of Pauline' and if you can't take it from there—it's too bad."

My mother permitted me to have a few dates when I was fourteen, provided she knew the boy and all about his family. We had to be home by ten-thirty or ring and give some very good reason why we would be late. My first serious date was with an old bachelor lawyer almost twice my age. We went to the same church and both his family and mine were delighted. As a lawyer, he was very articulate with my parents and his family were so afraid he would be "caught," as they put it, by a "flapper." They knew I was a stick and had been very carefully reared. I would fit in the family and do just what I was expected to do.

Since both families were anxious, I suppose it is one reason the romance did not flourish as it might have. He was too fat and always thinking of food. Those were the days of Rudolph Valentino, and the comparison was not too good. Years after Dick and I were married, he looked up from checking a sheet of bond prices and asked, "What did you and Randolph Hawkins have a fuss about?" I said, "I never had a fuss with Ran in my whole life." Still curious, Dick wanted to know what broke up the romance, for he said every time he made a trip to Jackson to see me, somebody went out of their way to tell him I was getting ready to marry Randolph Hawkins.

I laughed and said, "If I told you, you would never believe me." He insisted, and I told him we had been to a party over on the north side of Jackson where it is extremely hilly and the moon was simply gorgeous that night. He picked up my hand and held it as he usually did—as if it were a hot potato, and said, "Look at the moon, Thelma, it looks just like an apple pie." That put the kiss of death on the romance. Rudolph Valentino would never have mixed moonlight and apple pie! I suppose after that, Dick thought he should be chatty, so he asked if I had heard of old Mr. Price and his cotton money.

Mr. Price was one of those rare souls who had no trust in banks. Each year when he ginned his cotton he brought the money home in cash, and each year hid it in a different place. This year he had just bought his girls a new piano and hid the money in the bottom of the piano. They lived in a country house without screens. That night an old cat got in the open window and onto the piano and began walking across the keys. Mr. Price was sure his money was being stolen so he grabbed his shotgun and blew a hole straight through the new piano. Such a pity to ruin a beautiful piano! The banker had spent many a restless evening worrying over the terrific responsibility of taking care of other people's money—they do, and I should know—I was married to one for forty-two years.

Sessions' Store

General merchandise, groceries and hardware—truly it was a country general store, started before 1900, as a furnishing base for the plantations the Sessions family owned. Once a month the black tenant farmers came in for provisions for the month, and when the cotton was ginned and sold, the account was paid and the balance given the tenant. We had a good line of staple groceries. A usual order ran like this: Four twenty-five pound sacks of flour, four twenty-five pound sacks of meal, a fifty-pound can of lard, twenty pounds of sugar and fifteen pounds of coffee. Added to that was any material they needed or shoes.

Almost every tenant had from five to eleven children, so they needed a big order. Our hardware department was exceptionally good and included harness and saddles, pipe and pipe fittings, windowpanes and large pieces of glass which Dick could cut into any size or shape. I did, however, exact a promise from him that he would never cut a mirror as I am the most superstitious person alive. I lived in fear of breaking the compact mirror until we were with our best friends from Huntsville at a bankers' luncheon.

He told me whatever hour of the day or night that Janet broke a mirror, he was prepared to ride eight miles in the country to Crooked Creek so Janet could throw the broken pieces in running water. Some kind soul had told Janet if you put the broken pieces of mirror in running water immediately, it will break the spell and the seven years of bad luck will not follow. I was relieved, as I lived near a big creek and could easily dispose of any broken mirror. I don't walk under ladders, or kill cats, and I try to stay in bed most of Friday the thirteenth. My family are embarrassed over my superstitions but I try to tell them I have known some really nice people who were superstitious.

In our store we also had dry goods, shoes and laces and a few medicines including Black Draught, Lydia Pinkham's Compound, castor oil, and turpentine. Our most popular seller was hair grease. The black people straightened their hair with it. The two brands we carried were "Dolly Dimple" and "Polly Peachtree." No grocery order was complete without a jar of one of these.

The store was operated for years by Dick's father and his partner, Mr. Otto Christmas, a man from Denmark who had come to the United States to seek his fortune. Mr. Christmas was ill and wanted to go back to Denmark, so when Dick was graduated from college and returned home, he fell heir to Otto's job. Then, after I married, I helped out by keeping the books, answering the phone and also did quite a lot of work in the Fire Insurance Agency that was located in part of the store.

We kept a circle of chairs around the office and the folks from out in the country could come in or shop, visit a while or wait for the rest of the crowd who had business elsewhere. We really had open house all day. Some of our good friends often went home to dinner with us, and the state insurance agents of the companies we represented all had dinner with us. Dick was then president of The Commercial Bank and he was in the bank until late in the afternoon after all banking was finished for the day. He came to the store to see the results of the store and insurance business for the day.

In the store we had two women clerks and one man, except during the war years when we had five clerks. One day during the war, a nice-looking young woman, Irma Thompson, came in and applied for work. She told me she had taught school in Findlay, Ohio. I assured her we did not do a big business and could not possibly pay her anything like she made in Ohio. She replied that her husband left at six in the morning and was gone all day and the only place they could rent was an upstairs apartment. This was most uncomfortable, and she did not know anyone in Madisonville and was distraught and lonely.

She said she would be willing to work for whatever amount the other clerks were getting. We were glad to have her, and never have I worked with a nicer person. We often told her she had shown us how nice Yankees really were. One day she waited on a young black man and she was determined to sell him a saddle which was the biggest sale one could make. She pointed out all the attractive features of the saddle and talked at length about the wonderful leather which would last a lifetime and the fine workmanship on it. When she finally slowed up for breath, he said: "Yes, Miss, that is all true, but I ain't got no horse." That ended that!

My only sister, Lois, and her four-year-old son, Monty, were staying with my Mom and Dad across the street from us while her husband was overseas in the European Theatre of War. Lois and Irma had become very friendly although Irma's husband was a corporal and Lois's husband was a colonel. Lois's little boy was Dick's shadow but he loved to be in the store as all the clerks made a fuss over him. Tourists frequently stopped in and asked for cigarettes which we kept for the family and our good customers.

One morning a man came in and asked if we had cigarettes and the clerks at the front said: "No." My young nephew standing nearby chimed in and said: "Oh, yes, we do have cigarettes," and dashed around the counter and pulled out two cartons. We told him we could sell only two packs to a customer and we handed him two packs. He put the money on the counter for the cigarettes. To one side, he put another quarter. I said in an icy tone, "You have paid a quarter too much." His reply was: "The quarter is for the little boy for telling the truth."

During the worst years of the Depression, cotton was a nickel a pound and I will never forget the old man who brought his gin ticket in for one five-hundred-pound bale. I put the twenty-five dollars on the counter, then put the seed money in another little pile. He just stood there and looked at it and finally shook his head and said: "Miss, cotton ain't nuthin', seed ain't nuthin', ain't nuthin', nuthin'." I sympathized with him, as my family had lost nearly everything they had. My father was in real estate and the bottom truly dropped out of that. We even delivered a spool of thread. Morris Credit drove the truck and his wife Hattie cooked three meals a day.

He was a giant of a man and ate like one. He

became ill and Dick sent for Charlie (Dr. Hopkins) and he found Morris had a blood pressure reading of two hundred and seventy. He told him to stay in bed ten days and then he would come back to check his pressure. Several days after, Dr. Hopkins was coming in town from a late call and saw Morris coming out of the black night club they called "The Hole in the Wall." Charlie pulled his car over to the curb and called Morris over and asked him why he didn't stay in bed the ten days as he was ordered. Morris rolled his eyes around and then innocently said: "Yes sir, Boss, but you ain't said nothing about the nights." He stayed in bed all day and had Hattie bring him a tray every meal but as soon as night came, he covered the waterfront.

Hattie and I had a system about company. When one of the state insurance agents whose company we represented came, or an out-of-town banker, we always invited them to lunch. I would ring Hattie and say: "Hattie, another," and she would ask, "Big or little?" This meant could we eat in the breakfast room with every-day china or was he important enough to get out the Haviland and set the table in the dining room. I almost always replied, "Little," as we always had a good dinner and, being Sessions, we always had a good dessert. The man usually was sitting near enough to touch while I was talking but I doubt if he suspected the conversation.

Morris continued to have high blood pressure, and a few weeks after his first attack, he suffered a stroke and died. I immediately began to see a small man whom the black people called "Deff John" as he was totally deaf. It was obvious that "Deff John" had taken Morris's place. Hattie always confided to me whatever was bothering her while I drank my

first cup of coffee. I went out to the kitchen long
before Dick was dressed and she stood in the doorway between the kitchen and breakfast room and
we talked—something she never would do in Dick's
presence. Two weeks after Morris's burial I noticed
she was very concerned and finally asked: "Miss
Thelma, how much does a 'force' cost?" I asked
if she meant a *divorce* and she said yes.

I told her Dick had gotten one for somebody on
the place the week before and it was thirty-four
dollars. But I told her Morris was dead and what
need would she have for a divorce. She then told
me "Deff John" had a lawful wife living in Louisiana so he thought he could marry in Georgia and
it would be alright but the lawyer had told him he
would need to apply for a divorce. I was stunned
at such fast goings-on as we were all so ultra-
conservative. I advised her to wait a year or even
six months as we just didn't do things like that. She
looked very thoughtful, then asked, "Well, Miss
Thelma, don't you think it is better to go on and
marry than to live any way?" I had to agree for
I had more than a superficial idea of what living
just any way was.

So they were married and "Deff John" kept the
yard just as Morris had done but he didn't drive
the truck. Things went on like that for more than
a year and Hattie had a stroke and died. Then Dick
and I started eating all three meals at my mother's
house just across the street. Mom had a wonderful
maid in Lucy whom she had taken when she was
sixteen and taught her to cook, to serve and to clean.

Lucy is still there keeping the house for me and
getting her same check every Friday. She has seen
me through much sickness and death; she will always

have a special place in my heart. Dick had died of cancer and my mother died a year later of a heart attack and the old maid aunt who had lived with us since I could remember died two years later of leukemia. After Dick's death, I realized I could not continue with the long hours the store exacted. I did not feel like taking the responsibility, so I sold all I could and then called the Salvation Army in Atlanta and asked if they would like to come get all that was left.

The man was very pleased and said he would be there that afternoon. He came and loaded it all in a huge station wagon and my forty-two years in the store business terminated. The store has now been made into a drugstore and I never pass it without memories of the many happy, busy hours I spent there. I never walk the streets of the little town that some black man doesn't ask, "Miss Thelma, how are you making it without the boss?" If he really knew, Miss Thelma is having a pretty difficult time. Time does not heal all things—it just takes the edge off.

The day of the old country store has passed and given way to the chain stores in many little towns but the thousands of us on the other side of sixty will always remember. Some, like I, will recall the store where I bought a dill pickle every day with my nickel-a-day allowance when I was in the third grade. I was supposed to buy a candy bar but I bought a pickle and the storekeeper threw in enough crackers to keep me from choking. One day the tragedy of tragedies occurred.

I dropped my nickel in the pickle barrel and was leaving the store crying when Mr. McNeil, who owned the store, asked what was the matter. Between sobs I told him I had dropped my nickel in the pickle barrel. He put his arm around me and said: "Oh, you can have your pickle and we will get the nickel when we drain the barrel." I was so happy and I told everybody in the third grade Mr. McNeil was the kindest man in the world. I hope now in the years that follow the old country store, somebody will look back and say, "You know that Sessions' Store was a real institution. These were good people—they worked hard and they didn't mind it."

My Mother-in-Law

No relative on earth has been as much maligned as mothers-in-law. But when they handed out mothers-in-law, I hit the jackpot for I had, beyond all doubt, the best one in the world. She was sweet and easygoing and always on my side of any discussion. Her house was not a mansion but a large, comfortable one, with furniture that showed she had raised four boys and a girl without too many restrictions. She always made you feel welcome and had the best food in the world. Cook, as we called Mary, who had cooked there fifty-two years, and her cousin Susie, did the housecleaning and Joe, the yard man, was much younger and he milked two cows, kept the yard and a good supply of wood cut for the big range in the kitchen.

"Mr. Jim," as I called my father-in-law, was much older than his wife, and both he and Dick called her "Miss Edna." I also said, "Miss Edna" and "Mr. Jim." Miss Edna was Mr. Jim's third wife, the first having died in childbirth, and the second one of tuberculosis, and neither of them had children. Mr. Jim was superintendent of the Sunday School at the Methodist Church for forty years. Everybody in his house not in bed with high fever must be ready to go to church when he cranked up the Model-T Ford on Sunday morning. He had a well-known habit of inviting any visitors at church to dinner on Sunday and sometimes there were as many as eight extra.

I would have been exasperated if Dick had done me that way but Miss Edna went home and quietly unset the table, got out sufficient extra leaves and set more places to accommodate the extra guests Mr. Jim had brought home. I have helped her do this so many times and marveled at the fact that she never seemed ruffled. Cook had baked two cakes on Saturday, and on Sunday had cooked eight or nine chickens and Joe froze a gallon of homemade ice cream, so with some five or six vegetables from the garden, there was always a bountiful and delicious dinner.

Miss Edna not only was an excellent manager and housekeeper but had good business ability. Her father, the old doctor, as everybody called him, had ideas far beyond his time. He believed women should be taught how to manage money and property. Consequently, he sent his two daughters to Soule Business College in New Orleans after their graduation from college. The fine and capable George Soule who still owns and manages the college, said, "The Woods Girls" were his first female students.

The Sessionses, or rather Mr. Jim and Miss Edna, had some thirty or forty acres of land behind the house and there was one of the prettiest ponds around on it. The colored Baptist church liked to have their baptismal services there. The minister, Brother Stafford, would come by and ask Miss Edna if they could use the pond the third Sunday. She always said yes but asked that he see that the gates were shut so the few cows in there would not get out. They were careful and there was never any trouble.

Miss Edna would never let any of us go down there for she was afraid they would think we came out of curiosity and she considered a baptismal ceremony in any religion a very sacred sacrament. However, when Sadie, Cook's cousin, was to be baptized, she asked us all to come. It seems when the candidates for baptism came up out of the water they either shouted, "Praise the Lord" or "Holy am I." The two just ahead of Sadie had used both of these phrases and poor Sadie, realizing she must shout something different, came up out of the water and to our great amazement cried loudly, "Christmas Gift." We all congratulated Sadie that Monday on the beautiful service and rejoiced with her that all her sins were washed away forever in the bottom of Sessions Pond.

In a very remote section of the county there is a settlement of people who are totally uneducated and a few of them can neither read nor write. They came into the store on Saturday and, as they always said, "made groceries," and I always visited with them. There was one couple, Jane and Wade Harris, who always brought me something they had made or something from the garden. They were so good-hearted and friendly, you couldn't help but love them. But with their work-worn hands and lined faces, you knew life had been hard for them. They had raised six children, some doctors, two lawyers. The girls had married and were living comfortably. They all came to visit every year but little dreamed the hardships their parents had gone through for them. Jane had a rounded humpback just between her shoulders and I often wondered if she had been dropped as an infant. Jane never mentioned it and I surely never asked. One day one of the neighbors brought in the news that Jane had died suddenly of an apparent heart attack and Wade had asked them to tell us he wished Mr. Dick and Miss Thelma would come to the funeral.

I very seldom attend funerals but I felt obligated to go to this one. The undertaker had some difficulty getting Jane in the coffin due to her humpback. He finally made the necessary adjustments and thought all was well. In that area, as well as the small towns around, they have the custom of opening the casket and the congregation files by for a last look at the deceased. Dick and I went down when our turn came as we always tried to do what was expected of us. Then, just as the procession was about over, one of the wires used to adjust the deceased came loose, and Jane popped up in the coffin. There was a stampede out of the church and her husband jumped out of the window screaming, "She's come back! She's come back!" Dick and I were among the few who remained in the church and the undertaker closed the casket and assured them she was really dead. A scant crowd followed to the little churchyard cemetery and witnessed the final part of the funeral. Wade's appreciation of our coming was touching, indeed.

On the way home, Dick paid me the greatest compliment ever. Dick was not a flatterer and this was the understatement of the year. He told me he would never worry about me in any circle because, with my insatiable love of people, coupled with my background and education, he believed I could hold my own whether it was with the intelligentsia or those who came in the store and had to sign their checks with an X. That compensated for the horror of the funeral and all the worries of that week, for a husband's compliment is the most important thing in the world.

Life was a dream prior to my having been tragically mugged, but now as I look back on the years gone by and know they were good years, I laugh at times, I cry a little, and certainly consider myself country folk as I lived in a town of less than two thousand population with thirty-five percent white and the balance black, for forty-two years. I am so grateful that I had precious parents, a wonderful husband, the best in-laws in the world and sweet friends who are genuine in their love. Life can't always be easy, but I leave you with Dick's favorite saying:

> *"This old world is mighty hard to beat*
> *A thorn for every rose*
> *But ain't the roses sweet."*

Uncle John and Aunt Annie

Aunt Annie and Uncle John were related to me on the Sessionses' side. They were a precious couple and everybody who knew them loved them. They lived in a funny house here in Madisonville that Aunt Annie had added on to every time she got in a building mood. They had two servants who had been with them for years. Patsy, the cook, had been there forty-five years and Stan Veal, the yard man, had been there the same period of time. Patsy was a wonderful cook and Stan made a great garden, milked the cows, did the hard cleaning and on Sundays pumped the organ in the Methodist Church for both morning and evening services.

I was the organist and the wonder is that I did not have a stroke during a service. Stan would doze off to sleep while pumping and you wondered if you could finish a hymn. Stan would revive and, realizing he had been asleep, would pump with such vigor the rear of the church shook. I often wondered if that organ came over on the Mayflower or shortly after. Finally, we got enough money to buy a Hammond organ with an electric motor. Playing was much easier on my nerves and those of both the choir and the congregation.

Aunt Annie was one of those rare wives who always got her way. If Uncle John didn't immediately agree to what she wanted, she went to

27

bed and remained there until she accomplished her purpose. Her stay in bed was no great deprivation as she had a steady stream of company and three times a day Patsy brought her trays laden with the most delicious food you could imagine. Aunt Annie and Uncle John had no children but Aunt Annie's sister died and left seven children which were divided among the family. Aunt Annie got the two youngest, Susie and Toni. Susie soon learned to wind Uncle John around her finger and Toni was Aunt Annie's favorite. She decided he was to be a fine doctor and they sent him to Tulane and later to study in Vienna.

He surely lived up to her expectations. Once when he had just learned to hunt he went out with a group of boys and a shot grazed his ear. Fortunately it did not hurt him seriously but it frightened all the boys in the party nearly to death. Somebody brought the news to Uncle John and he immediately got Dick to drive him home to tell Annie. Two of his friends who were with him when the news came offered to go also. When they got near the house Uncle John said, "Now, you boys just stay in the car, as I want to break it to Annie gently." Uncle John got out of the car and Aunt Annie, rocking on the front porch, got up and came down the walk to meet him.

Uncle John had a habit of raising his right hand and pointing his first finger skyward when he was about to make an important statement. As Aunt Annie got to him, his finger went skyward and he said in a very dramatic voice, "Annie, Toni has been shot." The men in the car could hardly believe that he was breaking it to Annie gently. Annie, of course, began to cry uncontrollably and Patsy got out the ever-faithful smelling salts and Aunt Annie began to quiet down. Toni enjoyed the attention that followed the accident and recovered too soon to suit him.

Aunt Annie was more afraid of storms and bad weather than anybody I have ever seen. Before Lois was graduated from college and went to west Texas to teach, my mother and dad were still living in Jackson. Aunt Annie went to Jackson to visit them and as my mother drove, she enjoyed showing off all the interesting places in Jackson. Each afternoon after lunch Aunt Annie went to bed and took a long nap. One day, soon after she had gone in for her nap, a summer blow of high winds and rain came up. Mom told Lois to go in Miss Annie's room and put the windows down. Lois went in and put the windows down but came rushing out and told Mom that Aunt Annie was not in there. Mom, a very positive person, said: "Of course she is in there, she has just been in bed a little while."

Mom went in and, sure enough, there was no Aunt Annie to be found under the bed, in the bed, nor in or under any other bed in the house. The closets were also checked, even the bathtubs. By that time, even my mother was baffled and, as a last resort, took another look in the big closet of Aunt Annie's room. When she got in the closet she heard a strange noise and after more examination, Aunt Annie was discovered crouched behind the wardrobe trunk Lois had taken to college singing, "Rescue the Perishing." They all breathed a sigh of relief that the storm was over. Aunt Annie had not perished and all was calm once more.

Uncle John taught a Sunday School class of young boys. Everybody wondered how he kept order as he shouted questions at them. There was no excuse for not answering questions. One Sunday morning he shouted at Dick's youngest brother Jim, and asked him what Peter did. He scared Jim so, he stammered and stuttered and finally said: "He was the man that made the cock crow." Not being especially religious nor a Bible student, I do not know whether Peter was the guy who made the cock crow or the one who walked on water but you had to tell Uncle John something.

Even as pious as Uncle John was, he liked his little nip of bourbon every night. Liquor was extremely hard to get in our dry county so he ordered a case from Atlanta. Just after he had put in the order he phoned the depot agent and told him he had some Sunday School books coming and to please call him when they arrived. A couple of weeks later the depot agent called and said: "Mr. John, you better come and get these Sunday School books, they are leaking all over the place." With a somewhat guilty air Uncle John went down to the baggage room to salvage his liquor. Only three bottles of bourbon were broken but the depot agent complained bitterly that "those Sunday School books sure made one hell of a mess!"

Uncle John had one of the most beautiful plantations around Madisonville in "Fairview," a place of some fifteen hundred acres. He raised cattle and grew cotton on part of it and the other had wonderful timber on it. He had a black overseer in Horace and a white manager and his wife, Mr. Pete and Miss Maude Stubbs. Uncle John went to the place nearly every day and sometimes took Aunt Annie and they spent the day with Stubbs. On one such occasion they went out, having told Patsy they would not be there for dinner—country folk have dinner in the middle of the day and supper at night.

After dinner, Uncle John and Mr. Pete went to check on the cattle and the damage the boll weevil had done to the cotton and Aunt Annie rocked and had a fine time with Miss Maude. After this was over Uncle John got in his Model-T Ford and came back to town. Patsy was getting supper ready and Uncle John asked where Miss Annie was. Patsy replied, "Lawd, Mr. John, she left here this morning to go to spend the day with the folks on the place." Uncle John's finger went skyward and he said: "Just left Annie in the country but I'll go get her quick." Aunt Annie had not realized it was late as she was still rocking, drinking buttermilk and talking about her friends who had died, most of whom had gone "under the knife."

That was the way Aunt Annie expressed it when any of her friends had to have surgery—they had to go "under the knife" and most of them ended up in Evergreen Cemetery. Uncle John got back to the country and got Aunt Annie and they arrived home a little late for supper but time made little difference to them or to Patsy. It was the end of a fine day, as most of their days were. They were devoted to each other, to the church, the community and their host of relatives.

Uncle John had one of the few automobiles in town at that time. He drove to town every day, parked the car and promptly forgot where he had left it. On Dick's hundred-dollar-a-month salary, we did not have a car so whenever I wanted to go anywhere I got in Uncle John's car and went and put it back where I had found it. My mother and dad had a car and I had learned to drive when I was in high school. One day I decided to go to the next little town, fifteen miles away, to a gift shop to buy a baby present.

For the only time in his whole life, Uncle John remembered where he had left the car, and when he found it gone sounded the alarm that the car had been stolen. Everybody in town with any type of vehicle was looking for it. An alarm to the adjoining counties had been sounded, giving the tag number and model and the sheriffs were advised to arrest the thief and jail him immediately. I drove back very happy and complacent over my purchase of a baby cap, totally unaware of all the excitement I had caused.

When I found out and realized how near I had been to being put in jail, I burst into tears and told Uncle John he should be ashamed to have me arrested. He said I should have told him, but I replied that I had never done so, and always put the car back where I found it. He put his arm around me and said, "Don't worry, it's all over, but next time you go out of town, just tell me." Believe me, after that experience, I didn't go out of the corporation for a long, long time. Uncle John and Aunt Annie were a wonderful couple. They helped many people and did so much good. I often think, if by the greatest chance in the world I ever reach that Golden Shore, as they always referred to Heaven, they will be among the first to greet me.

Bon Voyage

Grief does strange and terrible things to most of us. My husband died of cancer and, being childless, I went to live with my mother. Just as I was getting acclimated to that change, my mother died. The readjustment has been, and still is, bad. Thanksgiving and Christmas were sad—very much of a nightmare. There were only two children in my family—my sister, Lois, and me. She and her husband, Ralph Persell, have been wonderful to me.

It was Ralph who suggested that perhaps a trip to Europe would help and that if I wanted to go he would give Lois a trip and she could go with me. Lois thought it was a fine idea and she immediately started talking to travel agents. She had always wanted to go abroad and was quite thrilled. So, after much study of travel brochures, we finally decided on the American Express deluxe tour.

Never have two more naive and unsophisticated women taken off to tour Europe than Lois and I. We left New Orleans at 2:15 on Thursday, April 24 and flew to Washington. We had an hour and a half in Washington and boarded another plane for London. The flight was the only rough one I had ever experienced. I love planes and think the most thrilling part of a trip is when the pilot makes his last turn on the runway and begins accelerating speed for the takeoff. They leave the ground at 180 miles an hour and rise 1400 feet a minute until they reach an altitude of approximately 38,000 feet. It's all so smooth you hardly know you are moving. I have always liked to do everything in a hurry, so, flying is really my cup of tea.

It was very distressing that a woman on the plane suffered a severe heart attack. The stewardess asked if there was a doctor aboard and the man across the aisle raised his hand. The woman had failed to bring along her medication so the doctor really had a busman's holiday. He and the two stewardesses gave the woman oxygen all the way from Washington to London. An ambulance met the plane and they took her to the hospital. I never knew or asked the outcome.

We were really tired when we arrived in London. A representative of American Express who was to take us to the hotel spotted us right away. We probably looked lost and "country." He asked if we were Mrs. Sessions and Mrs. Persell. Lois, big eyed and tired, replied, "Oh, yes, I am Mrs. Sessions," and, pointing to me, said, "And this is Mrs. Persell!" I had heard of people who were so tired they didn't know their names, but Lois was the first person I'd ever seen that tired. We were tired and exhausted, so after he got us to the Grosvenor House we each took a sleeping pill and went to bed.

We awakened at 5:30 and went to dinner and then back and to bed again. The next day we were rested and fine. The following night there was a get-acquainted cocktail party. We enjoyed meeting the tour guide who asked that we call him Tony. There were sixteen in the party. Dr. and Mrs. Earnest Solomon (Sally and Sol) from Boston, Dr. and Mrs. Alex Hobson (Nita and Alex) also from Boston,

Mrs. Robert McLain (Clara Lee) from Tiffin, Ohio. Clara Lee's mother was a Spencer from Midland, Texas so she knew all of our Midland relatives out there, both were old-timers in Midland. The only difference was that the Spencers were very rich oil ranchers and the McGruders were not.

Mrs. Randolph McLain (Anita) was a sister-in-law of Clara Lee's and lived in Abilene, Texas. Both were lovely and more like Lois and me. Then there were Milly and Carl Singleton from Chicago. He was president of a packing company and her father, who owned the controlling interest, had made a trip to my home county contemplating buying the Stuart interests which were later sold to International Paper Company. Then there was Nell Holder from Birmingham and her daughter, Pat Lewis.

Pat had been married only a couple of years and was a darling girl. There were Percy and Nancy Moore from Asheville. They bought everything they saw and had the distinction of always being late. He had dark red hair and a temper that went with it. She was cute and she knew it. Then there was Isabel Taylor who was an interior decorator with B. Altman in New York. She wore the most beautiful clothes and was very attractive. She came originally from Texas, married young, and was divorced. Later she married a Philadelphia lawyer and he lived only a short time. With her came her friend and customer, Emily Rothchild. Emily was the oldest of the crowd as well as the richest. The grapevine of the tour reported that she was quite wealthy.

Our first stop was London and we were at the Grosvenor House across from Hyde Park for four days. Our room was lovely and, for the first time, we slept on linen sheets. In London we climbed the Tower of London, saw the Houses of Parliament, Westminster Abbey and Buckingham Palace where we saw the changing of the guard. Buckingham Palace is such a cold, formidable-looking place I don't wonder that the Queen spends most of her time at Windsor. We saw Eton College where students must be enrolled before they are born to be assured a place in the school. We saw Eton on the way to Windsor. Windsor is beautiful, situated on a high hill surrounded by beautiful flowers. Nearby, Queen Victoria had her precious Albert buried in a spot she could see from her bedroom window.

We loved Victoria's crown which weighed only seven ounces. She suffered from agonizing headaches and could not stand the heavy weight of the crown. From Windsor we went to Hampton Court. The gardens there were beautiful beyond description. It was a palace favored by Henry VIII and, we were also interested because a large segment of the movie "A Man for All Seasons" was filmed there.

From London we flew to Paris and stayed at the Paris Hilton in the heart of the city. We were in Paris on May 1 and that, to the French, is like Labor Day to Americans. All the shops and beauty parlors were closed, so the shoppers on tour were disappointed. I loved the Eiffel Tower where we had a very elegant dinner one evening. Everybody dressed and it was a thoroughly delightful evening. Some had too much champagne but everybody had a good time.

In some way I had not been able to really see the Eternal Flame so when we left the Eiffel Tower, our tour guide instructed the driver to continue to circle the Arc de Triomphe until Mrs. Sessions had seen the Eternal Flame. This he did and I was grateful. In Paris we saw the Louvre, Notre Dame Cathedral and Versailles. Then, on our last night, we went to the Lido—and, if you are looking for something "risque"—it will suffice. The dancers were really topless. In fact, a few strands of beads constituted their entire costume. My eyes were so big that one of the doctors across the table said, "Thelma, Madisonville was never like this."

Paris was a delight, except that our local guide was a bit belligerent. The French like our American dollars but they don't like us. This guide was quite different from our darling Emily in London. Emily was born in Poland, spoke five languages, and was most charming. She sympathized when I was disappointed in not having seen a marker on the exact spot where the Magna Carta was signed. She explained the exact spot was impossible to know but it was signed in the Meadows of Runnymede which we saw on the way to Windsor.

From Paris we flew to Vienna and the charm of this wonderful city cannot be described. We took a lovely ride out across the blue Danube. We saw the homes of Strauss, Schubert and Mozart. Everywhere we heard Strauss waltzes. Our guide explained that Mozart was so poor when he died that a public collection was taken to buy him a coffin. Even then they were unable to get enough for a coffin so he was buried in a mass grave. Years later, when his work was recognized, the body was exhumed, supposedly Mozart's, and a fitting and beautiful monument erected in his memory.

The people of Vienna, with its cultural background, have a charm and friendliness all their own.

Our hotel, the Bristol, was truly "out of this world." We had a powder room, a large bathroom (with a towel warmer), a bedroom with walls done in gray silk damask, matching drapes, and a beautiful crystal chandelier. We felt too elegant for everyday American tourists. The sheets on the beautiful inlaid beds were linen damask. We had linen sheets in London, but my best tablecloth wasn't as pretty as the Vienna sheets. The dining room in the hotel was paneled in mahogany and each table held an arrangement of pink carnations. Thank heaven, artificial flowers have not made their entry into European dining rooms.

The food was wonderful and beautifully served. I gained five pounds on the delicious rich pastries, but it's worth getting a new girdle—they were so good. We admired and bought elegant petit point bags and I bought a dress. Never having traveled, I underestimated how many dresses I would need.

Truly, Schonbrunn Palace was the loveliest of the palaces—not as ornate as Versailles—but beautiful and so immaculate. Their economy differs from ours, as our guide told us that the highest paid teacher there gets $150.00 a month. The guide had just bought a five-room apartment in an apartment house in a fine section of the city for $3,000.00.

When I try to make ends meet on the first of the month, with a deluge of bills, I wish I could move to Vienna. Maybe my ledger would show black—not red.

The Austrians wear pretty shoes and there are several shoe stores on every block. They are proud of Franz Joseph and the Empress Elizabeth and the Hapsburg Palace is the loveliest of the palaces visited.

Lois and I took a trip to the Vienna Woods. We felt as if we were again seeing "The Sound of Music." On a beautiful mountainside nestled a convent; the site of the convent had been the hunting lodge of the Emperor Franz Joseph. When the Emperor learned that his son, who was married and the father of several children, was infatuated with his young mistress of eighteen whom he kept at the lodge, he was furious. In fact, Franz Joseph made life so miserable for his son that the son, in desperation, killed his mistress and himself. The Emperor had the lodge demolished and a convent built on the site. The convent takes only twenty girls and there is a long waiting list of applicants for entrance.

From Vienna we flew to Rome. All roads lead to Rome and truly it is the Eternal City. Our Cavalieri Hilton Hotel was on the outskirts of the city—on a high hill. Each room had a large sliding glass door that opened onto a balcony. From the balcony one could see across the entire city and at night it was like a fairyland. The room was a dream in a different way than Vienna's Bristol. The Hilton was brand new and most luxurious. The European hotels have a nice custom of coming in at night, turning down your bed, and putting your gown on it. They laid it out and then squeezed it in the middle. I had a bright red nylon gown and was always amazed that they knew which bed to put the red gown on. I asked Lois if she supposed somebody had peeped. But it's real nice to have everything ready for bedtime when you are tired.

The people in Rome are sweet and friendly. Our first day there Lois and I decided to go to the shopping center. We had learned that the hotel has a bus for their guests. We went, and as we did not see

the bus, I asked a lovely looking woman how often
the bus ran. She replied that she did not know but
would find out. She went over to her car and a man
in the driver's seat got out and came back and told
us it ran every twenty minutes. She said she was going into town and asked if we'd like to go with her.
We said we would be delighted, so Lois and I got
in the back seat. Lois introduced us and the lady
said she would give us her card, but that we would
know her by her screen name. It was Gena
Rowlands, the actress who plays in *Peyton Place.*
Her husband is a producer and they were there making a movie. She was most gracious and lovely. Her
mother had come from Arkansas and her father
from Wisconsin, but they had lived the last five years
of her father's life in New Orleans. The man who
drove, whom we first thought was her husband, was
her driver. Pat Lewis, the youngest member of our
tour, kept asking us if we had seen Gena in the
lobby. She was quite envious of our experience. I
wonder sometimes why people were so nice to me—
whether I just look solid and substantial or whether
it's my gray hair.

Our trip to the Colosseum, the Roman Forum,
and the Pantheon made history come alive. "All
Gaul is divided in three parts" didn't seem nearly
so far away as it did in Latin classes. The Vatican
is certainly the high point in a trip to Rome. My
mother had given me a St. Joseph's Medal given
to her by one of her Catholic friends which had been
blessed by the Pope and I lost my purse containing
the medal several months after her death. In fact,
I had lost my purse so many times in Treppendahl's
Grocery that even the truck drivers would say when
I went in the store, "Miss Thelma, they found your

purse in the banana bin or with the pickles.'' But finally I lost it for good and the loss of Mom's St. Joseph Medal worried me more than anything else. So in Rome, I bought a St. Joseph and a St. Jude Medal.

Every Sunday at noon, the Pope comes out and blesses anything you hold up for this special blessing. We went out in the taxi with the two doctors and their wives. The taxi driver drove frantically and we had two very narrow escapes. I remarked that I wished the medals had been blessed before we got in the taxi as I doubted ever getting to the Vatican alive. The doctors and their wives were Jewish so they took a dim view of my interest in having the coins blessed. But we did get there alive and saw St. Peter's and the wonderful, saintly Pope Paul. I will treasure the medals and try to be more judicious in carrying them around.

Rome was wonderful and I put a coin in the fountain which the Romans say assures you that someday you will return. Nobody could help loving Rome—whether it was the people you met on the street, or whether you were an avid reader of ancient history. The gloves were wonderful buys. Via Veneto, the Broadway of Rome, offered so many fine shops. I have enough kid gloves to last the rest of my life but I will enjoy them. Then one shop offered the only indelible and kissproof lipstick I have known. For me, it's too late for kissproof lipstick, but I bought a supply just in case of a miracle.

The food was good, the hotel so comfortable and beautiful, that Mr. Hilton really learned what it takes to make a fine hotel—and the weather was so delightful I could have stayed in Rome forever. One night at dinner I entertained the crowd with the funny stories of things that had happened in the country store we operated for forty years in this little town in the Deep South. Most of our trade was Negro trade, as our county is seventy-two percent Negro. One of the stories was about the ten-word telegram our yard man received late one afternoon which read: "Meet your papa on the night train— he is dead." The old man had died in the Charity Hospital in New Orleans and they were sending his body here for burial.

There were many equally funny stories and everybody laughed so much that people around wondered why we were so silly. Then I admitted that they saw what one old-fashioned before dinner, and wine at dinner, would do. My tongue was loose at both ends. So, the next night, I sat primly and announced that I wasn't going to tell any funny stories and I wasn't going to act silly, but just act my age. Everyone insisted that I drink the old-fashioned and the wine as they hadn't laughed so much in months. Needless to say, I accepted!

From Rome we flew to Nice and from Nice we went by car to Cannes. There we stayed at the beautiful Carlton Hotel with the blue Mediterranean in the front yard. The people were friendly and the food and service were superb. At one meal there were four waiters hovering over a table where only six were seated. Lois was almost embarrassed over all the attention but they thought we were rich Americans and nothing was too good. It was a grand feeling if you are a lady for only a day—or rather, for three weeks. We traveled one day to Grasse— the city of perfumes. We saw the beautiful flowers from which the perfume is made and had fun smelling the stoppers of all the bottles. Loving perfume,

I couldn't decide which was sweetest so I bought several just to be sure I got the right one. Everybody loved that trip for we like to appear sweet whether we are or not. There is no spot on earth as beautiful as the French Riviera. That drive along the Mediterranean from Monaco to Monte Carlo is too beautiful for description. We enjoyed the palace of Princess Grace and her Prince Charming although they didn't ask us in for a drink.

Then to Monte Carlo—the place of places! I lost three times on the roulette wheel but when I located the slot machines, my fun really began. The slot machines will work for a franc and I was luckier than I usually am. At Las Vegas and other gambling places I have been I always put ten dollars in a separate purse and when that is out, my fun is over. But unbelievable as it sounds, I left the Casino at Monte Carlo two francs ahead. You see, I am a small-time gambler but it was such fun. If one of my oil wells turns out not to be a dry hole I am going back to the French Riviera and to Monte Carlo every day. I think I hold the world's record for dry holes so I do not anticipate an immediate departure.

From Nice we flew to Madrid. We had a beautiful room at The Luz Palacio which is a new hotel. The main advantage about Spain was that taxis were plentiful and cheap. Taxi drivers are so reckless that individuals planning to stay in Europe long and use taxis should triple their insurance. One of the people on the tour had a friend who lived in Madrid who told her of a very elegant and exclusive shop. We went there and I purchased a very colorful dress for my niece's wedding which was planned for June 15. Then, when I arrived home,

I learned that a lovers' quarrel had cancelled their wedding plans. My barn on my cattle ranch had burned and my best tractor was in the barn and it burned, too. I should have remained in Europe! But Madrid was interesting.

The art treasures at the Prado, the Royal Palace and the University buildings were lovely. At one night club we saw the real Flamenco dancers. I was surprised that most of these dancers are older people, but this generation has not learned or enjoyed the dances as their parents have. You must understand that many are the old gypsy dances and were dances for weddings, christenings, and wakes. They are really ceremonial dances. Many theories have been proposed to explain the use of the word "Flamenco," but so far, if the truth is told, no one has been able to say for certain why the popular songs and dances are sung and danced only by Andalusians.

Madrid is best known for its famous bullfights. I was anxious to see a bullfight and suggested that we go. Lois was horrified and emphatically said, "No." But Sunday was the fashionable day to go, so on Sunday morning I insisted that we go and finally offered to pay for the tickets if she would go. She finally consented but insisted she didn't want to go. I went to the lobby and paid twenty-two dollars for two tickets. Lois reminded me that I was critical of Anita McLain paying sixteen dollars for a ticket to the opera in Vienna and then I had no hesitancy about spending more for a bullfight, which was neither cultural nor enjoyable. When I bought the tickets, I also bought a book on the art of bullfighting.

I was truly going to be the sophisticated spectator. I read the book thoroughly and at one o'clock the car arrived to take us to the bullfight. Only a Sugar Bowl audience could compare with the crowd. The band plays a spirited march which heralds the beginning of the fight. Then the bullfighters and the matadors come into the arena. The bullfighters must prostrate themselves in the arena before the cape of the matador is placed on their shoulders. The bulls look like my Angus bulls, only somewhat smaller. The first bull came charging out and the capes of the matadors began to wave and the fight had really started.

When the bullfighter stuck the bull and drew blood to make him unable to put up much of a fight, Lois started turning pale. Then, when the fighter was able, with one stroke, to kill the bull instantly, Lois was ready to leave. I insisted that they had five more bulls to kill, but she insisted they would have to kill them without us. So, while they were displaying the dead bull around the arena so that there was no doubt that the matador had been successful, we were rushing for a taxi to take us back to the hotel. The next day our plane left Madrid for New York.

Europe, with its beauty, its grandeur, and its history was wonderful, but more wonderful still was to say "Home Again." And so we look back on a wonderful trip and a delightful group. Most of them had traveled extensively as had our darling Sally and Sol. They took me under their wing and I loved it. Lois asked Sol why he didn't go into general practice because he had such a nice personality and people could tell their troubles easily to him. To that, Sol replied, "My God, I did it for twenty-four years, and I heard enough troubles so

now I just knock them out.'' He is an anesthesi-
ologist. But if I ever get sick in Boston, Sol is going to have to listen again.

I am sure the others in the party are remember-
ing the happy days and lovely friendships made. And
our tour guide, Tony, is on the Isle of Capri with
his lovely young wife. So maybe the coin in the
fountain will beckon us to return someday. We shall
see!

My Aunt Lou

My Aunt Lou was *really* a character. Born the only child of wealthy parents who traced their family back to William the Conqueror, she enjoyed every advantage given to young ladies of her day. After her mother's death she and her father traveled constantly. She had been educated at The Sorbonne and each year after her graduation she and her father made several trips to Europe.

Aunt Lou's father was a Woods and all of the Woods were large landowners. Each of them had several plantations and raised cotton, sugarcane and rice. The Woods men were good looking and second to money, loved liquor, pretty girls, and a good time. But when they married they were model husbands and sent their children to the finest schools in this country and Europe. Those who studied medicine talked the old doctor, the head of the clan, into sending them to Vienna, the then height of medical training.

But to get back to Aunt Lou, or I should say, Louisa Wellington Woods. She was married in the old Episcopal Church her family had attended for generations. Opposites must surely attract, for she married Dr. Harry Wingfield who taught history at Louisiana State University. He was a very quiet, placid man with impeccable manners. He seemed happy with his charming, vivacious wife.

Although they had no children, Aunt Lou entertained often and lavishly in the big old-fashioned
house full of beautiful furniture, bric-a-brac and
Oriental rugs. She had inherited her mother's
jewelry, the three-carat diamond engagement ring,
the diamond cross and diamond bracelet. She loved
to wear all of these to her Colonial Dame Meetings
for they were so much admired.

After they had been married fifty-three years,
Uncle Harry developed lung cancer and died within
a few months. Aunt Lou was left alone but with
a host of friends and ample money from the Woods
that Uncle Harry had carefully invested in bonds and
put in their joint safety deposit box at the bank.
Although they lived well, Uncle Harry saw to it that
his wife's money was wisely invested. Everybody
thought a widow of seventy-eight would go out very
little and mourn properly. But not Aunt Lou. She
went to all the concerts and cocktail parties in Baton
Rouge. She soon made the acquaintance of a Mr.
Barry Stierman, who asked that she call him by his
nickname, "Sherry."

He escorted her to parties and was a constant
visitor in her home. He assured her that she didn't
look a day over fifty. Sherry told Aunt Lou he had
been in the investment business and would gladly
transfer her bonds to his box and examine them at
his convenience. He also persuaded her that the diamond cross and bracelet would be safer in his box.

All of this my dear, sweet gullible Aunt Lou
believed. They were married and he suggested that
a drawing room on the train to Chicago would be
more pleasant. So, with her fussiest ruffled blue silk
dress and her mink coat, they started on a journey
into a wonderful new life. As they sat in the draw-

ing room holding hands, he looked at her mother's ring and remarked that one of the prongs appeared loose. As he was examining the ring, the train stopped. He quickly looked out of the window and said he saw an old friend he had been wanting to see and would be gone only a few minutes.

Time passed and the train started. With never a worry, Aunt Lou thought he was possibly talking to the conductor and would be on soon. An hour went by, and when she went to look for him, it appeared he had not boarded the train. When she arrived in Chicago with very little money in her purse, she recalled that Sherry had assured her never to worry about money again. She took a cab to the hotel she knew best and had them wire Baton Rouge for money.

Poor Aunt Lou returned to Baton Rouge realizing for the first time that she was an old lady who had really been swindled. But she continued to attend parties and club meetings and to entertain as she always had. But at one of the meetings of The Colonial Dames at one of the hotels, she started down the steps in a hurry, missed a step and fell down a long flight of steps and broke her hip. The shock was so great, a heart attack followed and we received the news that Aunt Lou had died. My legacy was a lovely china clock, green with pink roses on it; it was a rare Ansonia clock and I cherish it to this day. The only thing is that it ticks so loud and chimes on the quarter hour, the half hour, and the hour. Sometimes in the still of the night when it chimes, I wake to wonder if Aunt Lou will ever find Sherry, her bonds, her ring, her cross and her bracelet. Knowing Aunt Lou I feel she will, but only Saint Peter will really know.

The Widow's Mite

As the casket slowly descended with the last red rose of the floral spray passing out of sight, the large crowd seemed to quietly leave the cemetery in small groups. In nearly every group someone was saying, "I wonder what she will do now, an admiral's widow who was already wealthy in her own right." One was heard to say, "She should have no worries, just fun, as she has no children, and no responsibilities and more money than she will ever spend."

With quiet dignity, the widow, Nancy Turner Lawrence went about the business of picking up the pieces, the many pieces that only those who have experienced widowhood can know exist. Nancy's friends were wonderful to her. They took her to lunch, to dinner and to an occasional cocktail party. In the cheerful image that she portrayed, little did they dream she always had the feeling of being a fifth wheel.

In her childhood home where she had lived since her husband's retirement and her parents' death, she was very much afraid to be alone. Only a few of her friends knew that when she went out at night she always left a twenty-dollar bill on the table in the hall and her friends waited for her to go in the house and see if the money was exactly as she had left it. If the money was perfectly in place, she flashed the porch light to signal that all was well.

50

All was well except the place where her heart was supposed to be felt like a brick and the empty side of her grandmother's four-poster bed tugged at her heart in a never-ending hurt.

Although Nancy had lived all over the world as the wife of a serviceman, first as the wife of an ensign fresh out of the academy, and on up the ranks to the wife of an admiral, her friends persuaded her to travel. Her first trip was back to where they had lived and visited old friends, then to Australia and New Zealand. They were all familiar places and brought back memories of the days Randy was with her and, with his protective arm and position, the world seemed wonderful. Her last big trip alone was a cruise around the world and as her trip became more hectic, so did her blood pressure.

The doctors warned her to slow down and even old Dr. Wallace, who had seen her over measles, whooping cough and chickenpox, said to her one day in desperation, "Nancy, quit trying to run away from trouble, ain't no place that far." But still Nancy kept taking shorter but more frequent trips. She seemed to be propelled by something that kept saying "Push on, things will get better." But for widows without children, things cannot get better. One source of pleasure to Nancy was the frequent visits of service people passing through her little town of Madisonville, Georgia, to a new assignment. They always had a meal with her and frequently spent the night. They talked late into the night of days gone by, of friends who had died, been divorced or still others, who were serving wherever the Navy called.

Then suddenly one afternoon, while she was entertaining the Guild of St. George's Episcopal Church, she slumped over in her chair. The dagger, which had hung over her head since she learned of her high blood pressure, had fallen. The doctors had little trouble diagnosing it as a fairly severe stroke on the left side. At the hospital in Madisonville, she had so many friends who called, but she could only smile and wave her one good hand. Finally she was permitted to go home in a wheelchair with the aid of a live-in nurse and her beloved Sally who had been with her mother since before she was born and had held her in her arms while her mother was dying.

Life continued as uneventful as life can be in a wheelchair, but as Nurse Fannie pushed her about, she touched each piece of furniture lovingly and remembered Randy's comment when she bought the handsome grandfather clock in Germany. "This will look great in an igloo in Alaska." The teakwood screen he had bought in the Orient, he had remarked, "How will this look in an adobe house in New Mexico?" He joked, but he loved each piece as much as she did. Then quietly in her sleep, the massive stroke came, and for Nancy her heartache ceased. She was buried in the little cemetery behind the church where she had been christened and married.

She and Randy had decided they preferred the churchyard cemetery to Arlington, so far away and surrounded as they would be by strangers. As the townspeople passed the Turner lot and saw the stone which bore the inscription, "Nancy Turner, Wife of Admiral Randolph Simms Lawrence, Born June 29, 1918—Died Nov. 6, 1980," they remarked how lucky she had been and what a wonderful life she had enjoyed. Little did they dream that could she have replied, she would have said, "It was only a widow's mite."

Jim's New York:
A Short, Short Story

Madisonville has had some funny folks in the years I have known it but if we could see ourselves as others see us, we would all be called funny folks. Our neighbor's son, Jim Thompson, was graduated from Washington and Lee and came home, we thought, to settle down. His other two brothers had gone in the hardware business with their father and we wondered if the business could stand a fourth partner. But soon we learned that Jim was leaving for Atlanta to work for E. F. Hutton & Co.

He was a success in the office, for underneath that jovial countenance was a shrewd businessman. After some months in Atlanta we learned that he had been given a promotion and sent to the New York office. When I called to congratulate him he said, "Oh darling, my day is not complete if I don't have a visit with you." Just how many old ladies he said this to, I imagine is quite a few. E. F. Hutton had reserved a room for him in a very fine small hotel until he found a suitable apartment he could afford.

After a few months in New York he had some friends from Washington call him. They were in the city and invited him to have dinner with them. They gave an address of a restaurant in Manhattan that he knew was not in the most desirable part of the city. However, he took the subway and went to the address they had given him. After a search of five restaurants and three bars, he gave up and started walking back to the subway. As he walked along a not-too-fashionable street of houses, a man suddenly appeared out of one of them and stood right in front of him, pulled open a knife and said, "Give me all the money you got."

Jim was unshaken and answered, "I'll give you all I have but I only have seven dollars." He pulled out his billfold, counted out the seven dollars, then jokingly said, "Don't you want my American Express card or my VISA? You could have a lot of fun until you get caught." As an afterthought he said, "This is a good leather billfold. Might bring you a couple of bucks." The man looked absolutely astounded and did not answer. Jim had not gone far on his sixty blocks back to the hotel when a taxi stopped and the cabdriver said, "Get in, and I'll take you where you want to go."

Jim got in quickly and inquired since when did cabs pick up passengers and surprise them? The cabdriver then informed Jim that a man down the street had paid him, told him to pick him up, and take him wherever he wanted to go. When they arrived at Jim's hotel, he turned around and asked, "How much money did the guy give you to bring me back?"

"Ten dollars," the cabdriver replied. Jim went in the hotel muttering, "Funny city, funny folks, this New York—but I love it."

Europe Again

To be truly sophisticated you must be able to say, "The first time I went to Europe," and then casually refer to "the last time I was abroad," leaving to the imagination of the listener the many times in between. For Lois and me it was the first and last trip. This last trip could not compare with the first; on the first we had only sixteen people, and on the last, there were over forty. The first crowd were all wealthy and had traveled extensively, while the second crowd had saved a lifetime for a trip abroad. Some were really not able to fully appreciate many of the wonderful things the various countries of Europe had to offer. One couple found out that Lois and I had been to Europe before and attached themselves to us and the woman kept talking about their mobile home. It was two days before I realized the people lived in a trailer.

We met at the airport in New York and the plane was two hours late. Everybody had become somewhat jittery as this was their first real long flight. We landed in London and, as before, stayed at the Grosvenor House. The cockney maids were difficult to understand, in fact, my sister said she understood the maids in Paris better than the ones in London. We did the usual things—saw Westminster Abbey, the changing of the guard at Buckingham Palace, the River Thames. We climbed the Tower of London and made the train trip to Shakespeare country. We may have gained more knowledge of this great man but we also got aching feet from walking over cobblestones.

One day while still in London we were told that there would be a night meeting of the Scottish Clan, an organization which listed the Queen as a member. They advised that the guests at the hotel could come and stand behind the roped-off enclosure to see the bagpipe band and also the Queen. Lois and I went down early and were standing in the first row. We got a wonderful view of the entire proceedings. Queen Elizabeth and her handsome Philip were near enough for us to touch. She is lovely looking and most gracious. I don't wonder that even the cab-drivers speak of "our Queen" with such admiration and loyalty.

The second night in London we went to the night club "Talk of the Town." A comedienne from the States was the entertainer for the evening. I always enjoy the old gal but all of her jokes were directed at the Pope and the Pill. Since ninety-nine percent of our tour were Catholics, they didn't crack a smile. I do not have children and am now far beyond the age, so it mattered little to me. However, I have always considered taking pills of any sort to be a rather personal matter. The food was delicious and Lois and I enjoyed the evening.

The next day we flew to Amsterdam and stayed at a wonderful hotel which was on one of the canals. The Chateaubriand and peach melba for lunch were wonderful, and we toured the city by boat. That night we had dinner at the "Black Steer" and had a wonderful evening. When we returned to our rooms, looking forward to a good sleep, Lois discovered the commode would not flush. We called the office and they sent an elderly man up and he worked about ten minutes and said, "I fix." Lois tipped him generously and he left.

Upon further examination, Lois noticed it was not fixed at all—still would not flush—so we called and reported it. They sent a young man with a huge box of tools and he worked until one o'clock. We were exhausted but the young man did a job of getting the commode to work properly and Lois tipped him also and at last we could go to bed. An experienced plumber could make a fortune in Europe as I do not know of a country that would not welcome him with open arms.

We went by train from Holland to Switzerland. We had reservations at a hotel high on a mountain which had once been a castle. It overlooked the city of Lucerne and Lake Lucerne. The people are friendly and speak both German and Swiss and understand if you want to buy something. We had a beautiful room with a balcony and a private bath. On the long side of the tub, pipes were placed every two inches. The first morning I went in to take a bath and could not get a drop of water. Lois called the office and they sent a man up with a wrench. He worked a while and still no water. He then went down and brought up the biggest wrench I had ever seen.

He finally got the water to run, and Lois had him show her what to do. Lois, the wife of an engineer, knows more about tools than I, the wife of a banker. That night we had dinner in an attractive cellar dining room. After dinner we had a fondue party and were entertained by Swiss yodelers. The next day we again traveled by train to Venice.

We sailed down the canal to our Hotel Danielle. It was a very old hotel but quite luxurious and beautiful. We had dinner on the terrace and later took a gondola ride down the canal. I must say I am not overjoyed by canal rides as they all smell terrible. The one in Venice had a dead pig floating about in the canal which made you wish you could wear a gas mask.

We went from Venice to Florence and stayed at the Hotel Villa Medici. We had dinner on the roof garden and it was lovely. Then we went to the leather school operated by the monks. We bought letter openers, bookmarkers and Lois and I both bought beautiful purses. Gilda was our guide on this tour of Florence. She took us to the cathedral where we saw the Statue of *David* by Michelangelo, who was only twenty-six when he sculptured *David*. As a young man, strength abounded, and Michelangelo was a lover of the body as a symbol—not sex.

From Florence we went to Rome—all roads truly lead to Rome and we again stayed at our best-loved Cavalieri Hilton. The first place on the tour in Rome was the Vatican and Sistine Chapel. We also saw the *Last Judgment* containing 310 figures.

Michelangelo gave us *David, Moses, Pietà* and the *Last Judgment,* and as you know, painted the Dome of St. Peter's. Michelangelo, with his wonderful talent and dedication to art, never had a friend. His mother died when he was six and he withdrew from the world and became engrossed in painting and sculpture.

That night we went to Hosteria Doloroso for dinner and went on a night tour of Rome. Sunday we had lunch at Casino Valadier. Our guide took us to the Colossum and Roman Forum. The arches in Rome are particularly beautiful. Each conqueror erected an arch to himself and I think the one to Constantine is the most beautiful—that was the first time the city of Rome became Christian. I persuaded Lois to go with me to the Catacombs and the damp, clammy, spooky feeling was terrible. That is one trip that will never be repeated.

From Rome we went to Nice and stayed at Hotel Negresso. After a day in Nice our schedule was to fly to Cannes. As Lois and I were leaving our room to go for breakfast, we put our bags out for baggage pick-up. We saw the couple in the next room standing in the door. They were real hippies and they watched us until we got on the elevator. It made me quite uncomfortable. When we arrived at the airport, the tour guide announced that four bags had been stolen. One was mine and a couple from Detroit also had their bags stolen. They immediately began to list the items in the bag and came up with the astounding amount of forty-nine hundred dollars.

They asked me if I had that much and I told them I didn't think so. The guide was very upset and when he asked me if I had anything valuable in the bag I replied, "Yes, I had the most valuable thing I own in the bag—my Instant Coffee." I take instant coffee all over the world and you can always get an adapter in any hotel if you are aggressive enough. Four days later the bags were sent to Paris. It was the only time on the trip I had locked the zipper of the tote bag. They had cut across the entire bag and it was one grand mess. I threw out the coffee, fearful that I might get a taste of LSD and take a "trip" not on the tour.

When I asked the little Frenchman at the desk

what on earth I could do, he very reassuringly said,
"Oh, Madame, I will get a little rope." He disap-
peared and returned with a rope. Lois had made me
buy a whole new set of luggage for this trip and I
traveled in style but returned with my bag securely
tied with a rope. It was easily distinguishable because
it had the distinction of being the only one tied with
a rope.

We boarded a plane from Nice to Paris and
again stayed at the Paris Hilton. As the afternoon
was our own, Lois and I went to the Louvre. We
took time looking at the wonderful, priceless pain-
tings, particularly the Mona Lisa. While we were studying her features, a lady rushed in breathless and
said to an attendant, "Quick, the Mona Lisa, we
are double parked." She took a hasty look and rushed out with the same rapidity with which she came
in. Little did she dream that Mona was a real
person—the wife of a very wealthy and prominent
businessman in Florence. She had just lost a child
and it seemed nothing could console her. Finally her
husband decided that having her portrait painted
might divert her for a while and since it turned out
to be such a masterpiece, she was pleased. This, our
friend who was double parked, missed.

Lois and I concluded that we were accustomed
to instant coffee, instant oatmeal and now, we were
seeing instant culture right before our eyes. Paris
has so much to offer of interest, beauty and culture.
Notre Dame, the Queen of Cathedrals, with its
tremendous medallion in every color of stained glass.
The guide told us that when it was built hundreds
of years ago many people could not read. The blue-
and-green figures on one side and the rose-and-
orange on the other, told the story of Christ, the

Holy Mother and the Apostles. The wonderful Eiffel Tower, built in 1889, the Ecole Militaire, counterpart of our West Point, Invalides, where Napoleon is buried and the great Arc de Triomphe built to commemorate Napoleon's victories. And then there is the Eternal Flame by the Tomb of the Unknown Soldier, as well as the breathtaking Versailles.

On our last night in Paris, Lois became ill with some sort of flu. She had a chill and high fever and refused to let me call the doctor. I was terrified but I had dinner sent up to the room. I spent the evening we had planned to go to the Follies writing dozens of cards Lois had bought all over Europe. The next day, after two cups of strong coffee, Lois managed to get up and to the plane and we flew back to New Orleans. I was never so glad to get back and hand Lois over to Ralph as she really had a bad case of flu. In this age of travel people are bored with tales of trips and I have probably bored you too long with this.

But now, after being mugged in New Orleans, and two unsuccessful hip operations, my travels will be armchair travels, but we do have wonderful memories of some funny, some interesting, and some sad people we met. I am like Will Rogers—I love people, and Dick always said if he put me down in the middle of Africa, in less than a day, I'd find somebody who was in college with my sister or lived next door to my best friend's mother. The memories of this second trip we will always enjoy. Each time you go to Europe new vistas are opened and you realize what you had missed. If only I could walk, I would go again, and possibly bore you again— but I think you are safe.

Hawaii

My sister Lois is the one who loves to travel, and she initiates all the trips we take. After the first trip to Europe, she insisted that we go to Hawaii as all of her friends had been there. I agreed, and she immediately started making plans. I told her I would ask one thing especially and that was that she get a reservation at the newest and swankiest hotel on Waikiki Beach. For years in Madisonville I had been saturated with ancestors and antiques, and since I have a great many of both, I do not want to add to the collection of either. So according to that request she got a reservation at the Ilikai which fulfilled my every expectation.

Our flight from New Orleans to San Francisco was delightful, however, things changed when we boarded the plane for Honolulu. It was filled with wives and children going to meet their soldier-husbands and fathers in Honolulu on rest and relaxation. All of the wives were bringing their children to see Daddy. One lady had three small children as close together as nature would permit, and they fought up and down the aisle of the coach. As soon as the stewardess separated them and she turned her back, they were up and at it again.

The lady in front of us had twin boys, eleven years old. One of them had the most awful nosebleed I had ever seen. I have never had a nosebleed and did not know much about them, but this child's nose gushed blood like a fountain in spite of the ice bags the stewardesses used. That went on until the boy looked white and pale and drowsed off to sleep. Another woman had a babe in arms and the child cried all the way from San Francisco until we got nearly to Honolulu and then the poor little thing became exhausted and went to sleep. I could not help wondering just how much rest and relaxation the poor fathers would get.

A woman near the middle of the coach talked in a loud voice about all the things she had told the Colonel she would and would not do. Poor Colonel —if he met all her demands, I presume that would be one of his worst assignments. I punched Lois, whispered and asked her facetiously why she did not join in the conversation as Ralph was retired as a Lieutenant Colonel and she, too, was a Colonel's lady. Lois is one of the few Army wives that rank did not affect, thank goodness!

When we landed in Honolulu we were transferred to a big bus and each person discharged at his respective hotel. The Ilikai was wonderful and it had a large fountain in the center of the lobby. In the evening, Hawaiian musicians would play and those who had partners would dance. There was a glass-enclosed elevator on the outside that went up to the cocktail lounge on the top floor. Lois and I went up each evening and enjoyed the cocktails and the wonderful view of the blue Pacific. The beautiful moonlight over the beach would make even a lonely widow romantic as well as a woman whose husband was across the ocean.

The day after we arrived in Honolulu I called a lady who had done quite a lot of genealogical research for me on my father's fine old English heritage. She and her husband were living in London at that time but after his death she moved to the Islands. She invited us to have lunch with her the next day and thoughtfully told us that she was a very tall lady and also would be wearing a white dress. She would meet us by the pool at twelve o'clock.

She arrived at the exact time and we had a most delightful lunch and drive. When we got back to the hotel we checked our schedule and found that the travel agent had sold Lois two island-hopping tickets. These were one-day trips and we were to fly in a small plane. We immediately tried to cancel the trip but the agent refused. We concluded that rather than lose eighty-five dollars per ticket, we would risk death. Many of my friends have small planes and love them, but I have always wanted a big one that flew higher.

That night Lois set the alarm as we were to be picked up at six-thirty. We went to bed very nervous and every few minutes one of us would say quietly, "Are you awake?" and the other would reply, "No sleep yet." At last the alarm went off and I jumped out of bed and was sitting on the floor with one stocking on when I glanced at the clock and it said, "Three o'clock." I said, "Lois, what time did you set this darn clock for as it's only three o'clock." She remembered she did not have her glasses on, which accounted for the mistake. I went back to bed and she set the clock for five and we spent two miserable hours. At five we got up, dressed and went to the dining room for breakfast.

I hate early rising as I am not a morning person and I cannot go anywhere without two cups of strong coffee and a little breakfast. The bus picked us up promptly to take us to the plane for this island-hopping trip. All of my plane travel has been enjoyable but I cannot say that for this trip. It was a windy day and the plane that accommodated only fourteen turned every way but right. Lois brought along a new bottle of Dramamine and as everybody on the plane but me got sick, she passed the bottle around. Everybody took a pill and a little later, another one. We flew over one island low enough to see an active volcano which made you anything but comfortable. The pilot announced that we were going to fly over the island with the big leper colony on it. I asked quickly, "Do we have to land there?" I was very much relieved that we did not, as I have always been terrified of any skin problem.

On one very beautiful, isolated island where we had lunch at a very luxurious hotel high on a mountaintop, the young doctor and his wife who were sitting in front of us on the plane said so happily, "Tomorrow we are coming up here to stay a week and get away from it all." Since I had lived for so long in a tiny town away from it all, I wanted to go where there was activity. That hotel, fine as it was, would not have been my cup of tea. At seven o'clock we landed back in Honolulu and never have I been so glad to get back. We were still alive and we had not wasted our eighty-five dollars.

After that tour we decided to do our other sightseeing in the city and at the pineapple groves. The International Market was most interesting and we bought quite a lot while we were there. After we returned to the hotel Lois kept talking about a tablecloth she was sorry she did not get for her daughter-in-law. I finally suggested that, inasmuch as it was not much of a trip, we get a cab, go back, and get the tablecloth. We called the cab, went to the Market, got the tablecloth and called a cab to take us back.

On the way back I happened to remark that I hoped our reservations to leave had been definitely confirmed as we were anxious to leave the next day in order to get home for Ralph's birthday. Quick as a flash the cabdriver asked "And has your trip to the airport been arranged?" We told him it had not been arranged as we were not sure about our reservations. He gave us a card with his name, the name of the cab company and his cab number and said he would call us at nine the next morning. Lois took her card and wrote our names, the hotel and the room number on it. By then I was frantic over giving a stranger all that information. I told Lois he could have our throats cut by midnight and I was certain he was a thug.

The next morning we were in the dining room at nine and missed the call. However, to confirm my suspicions that he was a thug, I called the cab company and asked to speak to him. He answered immediately and said he would be there in ten minutes to take us to the airport. He came promptly and carefully loaded us, bag and baggage, in the car. On the way to the airport, I casually asked if he had a family. He said he was a Korean and had hired a marriage broker who was trying to get him a wife. He also said he was still in school but would receive his Ph.D. the following week and had a job in New York waiting for him. Lois asked him what subject he had chosen for his thesis and he replied, "International Relations."

Lois gave me that "I told you so" look, and I

felt better for at least if we were murdered, it would be by a highly educated thug. We arrived at the airport and took the suitcases up to Customs—much to my great amazement. Since Hawaii is our fiftieth state, I had not realized one's bags had to be searched to be sure you were not bringing out any fruits or vegetables. When I was fumbling in my purse for the key, the Customs man opened it with his master Samsonite key. Not having packed it carefully, my red nylon gown which was right on the top, rolled out, to my great embarrassment. He picked it up in a very gentlemanly way and put it back in my bag. Lois had been more careful with her packing. We thanked our Korean friend graciously, tipped him well, wished him the very best of everything, and boarded the plane to begin our journey back to the greatest part of the world—the Deep South.

Natchez on the Mississippi

The small town of Natchez sits proudly on the banks of the Mississippi River. It is a town of wealth, culture and charm. Years ago when there were only a few millionaires in the United States, Natchez boasted of having over half of them living there. Cotton was king then but since it no longer is, the oil industry has taken its place. Our tourism is a big business, started in 1932, when the Garden Clubs of America met in Natchez. Since the spring had been very cold, there were no flowers.

The capable and lovely Mrs. Balfour Miller said, "Since we have no gardens to show, why not open our homes and show them our beautiful and rare antiques!" They did this and the Garden Club ladies were more than delighted with the gracious hospitality shown them. Now Natchez has three garden clubs and offers several pilgrimages every year that have grown into a thousand guests a day on some of the tours. The strange thing is that some of the same people return each year. We have some tourists who are extremely well informed on both furniture and crystal.

My sister and her husband are the fifth generation of his family to live in the lovely antebellum home called "The Towers." We have been asked some unusual questions and as I receive in the dining room I try to make their visit enjoyable but am sometimes at a loss to answer questions. Last year one lady looked around and asked, "Is some of this furniture second-hand?" I replied it was probably tenth hand; it had been handed down so many times.

The prize question was asked at Stanton Hall, the magnificent headquarters of The Pilgrimage Garden Club. After the hostess had shown a group the downstairs area, she took them in the back parlor where there was a full length portrait of Katherine Miller and one man asked, "Is that Auntie Bella?" At "The Towers" one evening, the hostess who was receiving in the big bedroom across the hall rushed over to me and said, "Tell me quick, what kind of an engineer Ralph is, as a lady wants to know if he runs a train out of Natchez." My sister was standing nearby and she remarked that when Ralph ran a train, she would be sure not to get on it. To set the record straight, my brother-in-law, Ralph Persell, is a chemical engineer. I presume when she looked at the beautiful chandeliers and priceless antiques, she felt certain that he had robbed a couple of banks. A good part of the furniture came from Lois and my family.

After the tour, all of the homeowners have a little party for the hostesses who have received and, of course, their husbands are also included in this party. My sister had acquired the unusual habit of inviting the last guests in the house to join us for the party. We have met some truly delightful people, and one of the most gracious notes of appreciation she has received was from a Jewish couple in New York City who wrote they were delighted to be treated as guests and not as tourists.

Last year one man on the tour said to me, "Well, you are in the same place, telling the same story." I quickly replied, "Yes, but I do have on a new dress." Another man walked over to me and asked me how old I was. I replied that I was a hundred years old and he thought I was well preserved for that age. Some of the tourists have asked how long it took Natchez to hang moss on most of the trees. They little dreamed that Mother Nature had been doing that a long, long time. The Natchez Garden Club has a very beautiful headquarters called "Magnolia Hall." They have lovely hostesses and make a tour quite a treat.

Almost all the houses have a ghost and "The Towers" has several. Aunt Kate had a heart attack and died when the Northern troops took over "The Towers," as it was within the Federal Fortifications. When anybody in the house is ill, she returns and knocks on the outside wall. When someone goes to see about the knocking, all sounds stop and you hear it on the other side of the house. That is usually a sign that death is imminent.

Rumor has it that General Grant was so furious over having to come to Natchez that he kicked the marble hearth in the parlor. It is cracked but who knows who the guilty one is? He also was said to have ridden his horse up and down the hall of "The Towers" and vowed he would come back and ride up the hall every Christmas Eve. We do hear hoofbeats on Christmas Eve but upon examination we find neither the horse nor the General. In researching material, I attempted to find the name of General Grant's horse. Everybody knew General Lee's "Traveller" but it appears General Grant used several horses.

"Magnolia Hall" also has a ghost who returns often on moonlit nights. One of the daughters of the former owners of the house had fallen madly in love with a young man from Paris who was in Natchez on business. He was in love with her and they planned to be married. His business took him unexpectedly back to Paris. However, he wrote and begged her to come to France and they would be married. She packed her trunk and went to Paris, radiant with wedding plans.

To her great surprise she found him a different person in Paris and he did not want to marry her. She came back to Natchez brokenhearted and each evening would play the harp and sing the love songs they had sung together. After a short time, she suddenly passed away but on moonlit nights the harp can be heard and a faint sound of the love songs of long ago. When some of the family went to the drawing room there was no harpist and singing had stopped.

I am wondering if in the years ahead one of the future generations will see General Grant and his horse in the hall at "The Towers" on Christmas Eve. I hope someday you will find your way to this interesting town of Natchez and enjoy the warmth and graciousness of the people. To those who have visited us, all words are faint, and to those who look forward to coming, "no words can paint."